To Giulio
and Guglielmo,
with love.

IN THE LIGHT OF A FALLING STAR

Written by

Claudia Ravaldi

Illustrated by

Flavia Zuncheddu

Once upon a time, there was a beautiful old stone farm, surrounded by yellow fields and green of nearby woods and gardens. It had white walls, large windows with shutters painted green and a bright red roof. In front, a veranda faced the dusty air in which a prosperous garden of ancient trees and wild flowers bloomed.

Not far away ten milking cows and four horses slept and ate, lazily and serenely, to and fro from the stall to an old barn. Twelve egg laying hens, a stout and proud cock, two shepherd dogs, six funny geese with long necks, an old goat and a numerous family of multi-coloured cats also lived happily in that farm tucked away in the green fields.

Everyone moved freely in this immense space, eating, meandering and resting. Every evening at sunset they all gathered together under the stall's porch to watch the spectacular shift from day to night. Once the first star peeped out, everyone, apart from the cats, who delighted in catching mice and bats, went to sleep.

One warm May evening Mary, Mummy cat, was lying out on the grass while around her Oscar and Kitty played chase and ambush, and their Daddy, a grand black and white tabby cat named Oliver observed them proudly and knowingly.

Oscar and Kitty were two naughty, playful and independent kittens, who also needed hugs and affectionate pats. Every evening, before going to bed, they rubbed their little noses affectionately on their Daddy's head, then hugged their Mummy Mary who licked their ears and purred sweet words.

Oscar and Kitty became more and more excited in recent days because in their Mummy's tummy was a little brother who was going to be born very very soon. Being twins and the first born, they didn't understand what it meant to have a little brother! So they were excitedly curious and a little guarded... since they couldn't imagine what it would be like to have a baby in the house. What was going to happen to them, now that they were going to become older brothers?

Their heads, giddy with thoughts and worries, spun faster as their impatience grew. Oscar chased after Kitty behind the haystacks saying:

"Let's hope it's a boy,
so we can play fights!"

And Kitty exclaimed:

"Oh no! I want a girl,
so we can sniff flowers and chase
after butterflies together!".

"It's going to be a boy!!!" teased Oscar, hissing and arching his back. "It's a girl, I'm sure, I'm sure!" hissed back Kitty, baring her sharp little teeth and pulling her ears back. She was so angry, she rolled in the dirt until her shiny coat was covered in mud and dead leaves. Mummy Mary, while waiting for her new born to enter the world, watched these scenes with amusement and joy. Only a few more days to come and her new baby will finally be born. Mummy Mary wanted a big family and Daddy Oliver purred quietly into her ear "We'll have at least eight children, four boys and four girls, who'll scamper around us filling our lives with joy". Cat Mary and cat Oliver enjoyed planning and dreaming about a new and bigger house, maybe besides the sea or maybe in the city "So every morning our children will have fresh fish for breakfast", Oliver added, enthusiastically. Mary with tender half closed eyes gazed lovingly at her husband. She then stretched her body out and looked at her tummy that was so big and changed shape when her little baby inside stretched for space.

Oscar and Kitty split their sides with laughter, watching their Mummy's tummy make so many funny shapes, and with their paws, they tried to chase their baby brother inside.

"Carefully, your brother is very delicate, you could hurt him" said Mummy Mary, when the kitten jumped on top of her tummy to catch their brother.

"Why?" asked Kitty, curiously.

"Because kittens inside the tummy and also when they are just born are tiny and fragile and we need to protect them."

"Why?" Oscar insisted,

with his little paw suspended in mid-air.

"Because they are little and fragile and they could easily get hurt."

"But I didn't mean to hurt" said Kitty.

"Neither did I" added Oscar who was becoming a bit fed-up with his little brother in the tummy. His little brother was getting a lot of attention and was stealing time from his Mummy, who had stopped playing with them and no longer chased after them in the rafters of the old barn or under the hay stacks. Under his breath he angrily exclaimed how boring and unwelcome was this new brother: "Let's hope he comes out quickly from Mummy's tummy so we can play with Mummy as we did before. Then when he grows up he can play with us."

Days passed quickly and Mary's tummy grew and grew.

Every time Zoe the goose passed behind the wood mound near Mary's basket, she always quacked: "How are you going to cope when this third kitten will be born? You already have two kittens to look after, someone will have to be sacrificed". It goes without saying that Zoe was a real sticky beak goose and she never minded her own business. Mary smiled and nodded, turning her head away. Kitty didn't notice those words, but Oscar instead froze and his whole body trembled from whiskers to tail: "What does 'will be sacrificed' mean? Is Mummy going to

send one of us away? I don't want to be sent away thanks to that stinky ball!". Just the thought made tears come to his eyes, and Oscar ran and snuggled up against his Mummy.
Daddy Oliver comforted Oscar by licking his head:

"Everyone will have a place in the family.

No-one will be sacrificed". But Oscar wasn't entirely convinced and still was afraid, especially when Cocca and Lina, the two old hens from the hennery, stared at him, shrieking with their crowing voices: "You are the older brother and you must give a good example: now that you are grown up, no more running around, you naughty thing!".

Just as well, at the old farm there were more reasonable and understanding inhabitants, who were over the world with happiness about the arrival of the new kitten and helped the two brothers to be serene and tranquil. Fred, the cart horse was always happy and optimistic, saying: "Where you can carry two you can always carry three! When your little brother is born I'll take you for a gallop right up to the river, where we can go trout fishing!" Hannah the cow, who was always crunching hay, added: "When the little one is born all the farm animals will organize a welcome party, and you Oscar will be able to play all day long in the barn.".
Oscar was happy, and started feeling more secure: "How fantastic, having a party and eating a big cup full of fresh cream just for me", as Flora the cow promised him!

Days passed by and still nothing happened. Everyone was becoming impatient. One evening when the full moon opened the sky and the air was warm, the sage owl Bridget was called to speak the truth. She was an expert on births and mummies. Posed on the fence, Bridget gazed upon Mummy cat's tummy and cooed: "The children must be kept away". Sadly, Oscar and Kitty obeyed, taken away by Fred the old horse who appeared less jovial than usual and walked very slowly, shaking his mane every now and then. "What's up?" asked the kittens.

"I'm tired, sweeties" replied Fred, looking at the earth.

"Why can't we stay?" insisted Oscar.

"Why's Bridget so serious, and why doesn't she want anyone near her?"

"And why can Daddy stay?" continued Kitty, angry that she was forced to stay away. "Our little brother is going to arrive tonight?" both kittens asked in unison. "Maybe, children, maybe."

That night the two kittens slept at Fred's feet, in the stall. They were curled up and purring incessantly thinking about the imminent arrival of their little brother. At sunrise, the following morning, Oscar woke up first and, to wake up Fred and Kitty, he started to run and jump and skip from one hay stack to another, meowing like a madman.

"Come on, let's go, let's go!!!! Let's run and see Mummy, maybe he's born. Come, hurry up, we haven't got a minute to lose!!"

Fred got up slowly.

He saw Bridget fly away at sunrise and when he called to get her attention, she didn't reply but shook her wings slowly slowly.

Oscar and Kitty arrived under the veranda. In front of the wood mound Daddy Oliver was waiting for them. He smiled weakly and came up to them without saying a word, purring in long and noisy purrs. The kittens scarcely greeted him with the impatience they felt and their Daddy's silence went unnoticed, as they scampered upon the wooden mound, to reach their Mummy who was sitting on a branch immobile. She had a strange far away gaze, her eyes seemed empty without any warmth or expression. Her mouth was twisted in a grimace as though she was in pain, but the kittens couldn't see any injuries or bandages. They approached her slowly with circumspection.

Everyone was quiet, no-one spoke.

Further away, cooing to themselves besides the fence, Zoe the goose and Cocca the hen stared at the earth and were muttering to each other. Daddy Oliver after following them had turned away, determined to gather a large group of mice. No-one seemed to notice that the kittens had arrived, everyone was in their own little world, wearing dark and mysterious expressions on their faces. Oscar and Kitty lay next to their Mummy, and started to purr. Mummy gazed sadly upon them weakly trying to smile. At that moment the kittens took a longer look at their Mummy and saw that her tummy had disappeared!!

"Where is it, Mummy?" they asked in unison.

"It isn't there anymore. Little Tom has run away."

So it was a boy! "Fantastic" Oscar thought, without feeling completely happy about it. "He's gone away? How could that happen? A newly born kitten, that's decided to run away, how rude!"

"And where did he go?"

Kitty asked feebly as tears formed through disappointment.
"In paradise!" mooed Hannah.
"In the sky!" barked Pablo, the shepherd dog.
"It's part of the great circle of life, which we are a part of" meowed softly Daddy Oliver, with shiny eyes.
"Why don't you go and play, and let your Mummy rest?" whinnied Fred, firmly.
"Go and enjoy yourselves, and I'll bring you lots of cream afterwards!" promised Flora, as she nudged them away.

"Mummy, why are you so sad?"

whispered Oscar. "When is little Tom coming back?" while speaking he hugged his Mummy Mary, looking at her closely trying to understand better what was happening. Everything was very strange, no-one was happy for the little Tom, maybe because he ran away? "My little treasures, he won't be coming back, because he was ill, too ill."
"He was ill? How could that be? There must be a mistake!" Kitty thought "I remember seeing him twisting and turning vivaciously in the tummy and responding to my purrs".

"Little Tom was fine, there's no doubt about that! Was it Bridget the owl's fault? No, that's impossible. She was the best, even Daddy said so." Kitty started crying with confusion and sadness.

"But if he was as ill as you said he was, how could he reach the sky as you had told me?" Oscar, his head giddy with thoughts, asked. He just couldn't believe that his little brother had gone away.

Mummy cat started crying, quietly and everyone around her hushed in silence.

Everyone, except Gotta the old and wise goat.

"Little treasures, little Tom was weak and ill and couldn't live outside your Mummy's tummy and because of this he died, making all of us very very sad."

"But when's he coming back?"

Oscar still couldn't understand. It was really important to know, because he wanted to see him, he'd been waiting for this moment for weeks!

"Well, only little Tom's soul flew away, his body remained here" Gotta continued patiently.

But still Oscar couldn't understand: everyone was so silent and Mummy and Daddy were so different from their usual happy selves. Daddy was always so busy that he didn't have time to listen to anyone and Mummy even if she was there was so far away.

"This happens when we complete our voyage on this earth and a part of us goes away and the other part remains" Gotta sighed.

"And so where is he?" murmured Oscar. Kitty hidden under a cardboard box was crying softly. She didn't want to be seen, but she cried so hard that the entire box shook, and everyone could understand what was happening inside.

No-one replied.

he added disappointedly. Mummy Mary at that moment turned towards Oscar and with tenderness whispered: "If you wish we can go and greet your little brother together. Follow me."

A clamorous chorus of "Ooh.... Nooo..... But.... If....." from the geese and hens who were getting up from their nesting spot.

No-one took any notice, and Mummy Mary, followed by her two kittens approached the stall, behind the cows' drinking trough. There, above a little cushion of leaves and flowers, a little black kitten was curled up and on his forehead was a little white star. The little kitten had his eyes closed and his little paws were uncurled and restful. The little face was serene and he appeared to be sleeping.

Oscar went close to him observing his little brother.

"How beautiful" he whispered with a fine voice.

"What a beautiful tail. Who knows how fast he would have been able to run." added Kitty.

"He's so soft... but why is he dead?" asked Oscar.

"When kittens are too weak it happens." his Mummy answered feebly.

"Is it because of the punches?" asked Oscar, finding it hard to swallow. His heart was pounding and he was truly frightened.

One time, he remembered his Mummy telling him off, because he played too heavily on her tummy. Maybe it was his fault?

"So it's your fault!" screamed Kitty, hissing loudly and arching her back.

Oscar started crying in desperation.

Mary calmly reassured them:

"It wasn't anyone's fault, it happened and that's that. Now we must wait for the pain to pass, and say goodbye to little Tom."

The two kittens kissed their brother on the furry cheek and caressed the white star on his forehead; their tiny hearts pounding sadly. Now they felt very sad and were worried about their Mummy and Daddy. What was going to happen? Maybe Mummy will never smile again.

During the days that followed little Tom's death, Oscar and Kitty tried to be good, but inside they felt a tide of many different feelings and emotions. They wanted to run and jump, but then they thought that you shouldn't jump and run when your little brother has just died. They wanted to fight between themselves, but Joanna the goose in her shrieking voice warned: "If you start to fight, you will break your Mummy's heart" and so the kittens, frightened by those words tried to be as quiet and still as possible.

Every now and then Fred the horse and Hannah the cow visited them, bringing something nice to eat and playing with them.

Even though many days had passed,

but often she cried, especially when the hens Cocca and Lina returned from the nearby village gossiping about how the persian cat had just had a batch of kittens or the baker's cat had given birth to three strong and vigorous triplets with bright red fur.

Oscar and Kitty continued suffering a little, and wanted so much to help their Mummy but they didn't know how. Kitty embraced Mummy and Daddy, and they awaited those moments of affection with tenderness and love. Mummy Mary always smiled when she was embraced by her little kittens and her eyes lit up with joy even if it was only a flicker. Oscar missed his little brother and understood that his Mummy felt the same way. They saw him for only a fraction of time and afterwards Mummy couldn't embrace him anymore. How could they overcome this?

One day, after much thinking and rethinking Oscar had an idea and went to tell his Daddy about it.

At first, Oliver hugged him strongly and then said: "Let's do it, I'll help you, what shall we do first?"

"Come on, let's get the ladder!, it's a secret ok?, it's a surprise!" exclaimed Oscar, full of enthusiasm!

"You can trust me, you know that, don't you?" replied Daddy Oliver, as he got stuck into the job. Back and forth from the nearby wood to the tool shed, hidden from all, he gathered lots of sticks and pieces of wood, cutting down the young and tender reed like branches from the weeping willow and he worked day and night without stopping. It was almost sunset when he finally finished the job.

Oscar, went to the stall to call all the inhabitants of the farm leading them to the foot of a great huge oak tree, the oldest and biggest tree in the entire farm.

"Mummy, come up here, and you won't ever be sad again" said Oscar, pushing his Mummy towards the tree.

His Mummy looked at him curiously since she didn't understand.

Then she saw it, oscillating slightly with the evening breeze, the longest cat ladder she had ever seen in her life.

"You see Mummy" Oscar happily explained. "With this ladder you can get right up to the top. Once you are on top you can see the whole sky and the entire earth. If you climb up there, little Tom will see you, and you can greet him, and then you'll be less sad."

Mummy, moved by this gesture hugged Oscar and said to him:

"I love all my children so much.

When I see little Tom I'll give him your greetings."

As she spoke she climbed right to the top of the tree, her little nose pointed upwards.

Shortly afterwards, all were amazed to see the bright flash of a falling star illuminating the sky.

When it shifted from night to day, Mary descended from the tree and she lay next to her kittens.

"So Mummy, what did you see?" asked Kitty with hesitation.

"What did he say?" continued Oscar, quivering.

"He said that he loves you a lot and that he will always be with us, in our hearts, and will accompany us forever".

"And will he come back?"

"In the light of a falling star,
in the coloured arch of a rainbow
and in the sweet scent of Spring,
he will always be with us
and we will remember to look for him."

Having spoken those words, Mary and Oliver hugged their kittens and everyone began to purr.

Notes for parents and professionals

When a baby dies, the experience is so painful that it often becomes impossible to even speak or think about it. Very often no one knows what to say and noone seems to find the "right"(in a child's perspective) words. Usually, people prefer to avoid the subject, hiding the event or minimizing its impact by using phrases like "Don't worry, your mother will have another baby soon" or "The baby is better off where he is now", "Your brother was an angel and the Lord has taken him " and also "You have to be a good boy, because your mum is sad" etc.
Sentences like these, which can be meaningless and even offensive to some parents, might even be harmful to the other children in the family, who often start elaborating the loss on their own, with resources that may vary according to their age.

When a baby dies, other children, even very young ones, are aware that something has changed, primarily because the attitude of adults changes, some habits change and expressions and emotions associated with pain and sadness frequently appear. This event can occur in all stages of pregnancy or the post-partum period and older children often react in two possible ways. They might either start asking insistently why the belly is gone or when the baby is coming back (because no one has told them what really happened and everyone acts calm and relaxed), or feign indifference and silence, waiting for adults to explain. Adults frequently think that children are incapable of understanding death or facing the event without suffering serious consequences. Because of this over-protective attitude, children are often left out of the mourning process. As a matter of fact, children can approach the issue of birth and death with surprising clarity and ease. If the appropriate terms according to their age are employed, they are able to understand the event with the least pain possible. What can frighten children most is the ambiguity that surrounds adults on the subject. Since adults do not speak openly about death, it sometimes happens that different people will tell different things to children, who then receive multiple versions of what happened, often conflicting with each other. That, paired with the unusual atmosphere at home and the unavoidable changes in family habits (for example, due to a long stay of the newborn in intensive care, to early hospitalization of the mother or to intrauterine or crib death), intensifies their sense of confusion and disorientation.

Receiving or overhearing elusive or confusing answers, such as "It was for the best, because the child was unwell" or "Now the baby is in the arms of the Lord" or "Your brother has gone away to another house" or "Mommies' bellies are magical and sometimes they disappear, but then they grow back", may enhance the sense of loss and the difficulties that children encounter when having to deal with so many changes all at once.

Children should feel free to ask and obtain simple and consistent answers to questions like "Why is Mommy sad?" or "Where is my baby sister? When will she be back? Why is she dead? What happens to dead people?". If the family fails in dealing with the topic and uses confusing explanations, children might blame themselves for what happened and start fearing the same will happen to them or that parents too will "disappear". Sometimes children react to these fears and anxieties by losing previously acquired abilities (like using the bathroom autonomously, sleeping without a diaper, riding on the schoolbus, etc.) and incessantly claiming their parents' attention. In other cases, especially if children are of school age, they might start acting more responsible and "adult-like", for example trying to take care of their parents. A simple and straight-forward conversation about the death of a brother or sister, sharing emotions typical of mourning, and explaining what happens when someone dies through terms that are understandable for them, can make a difference and are an invaluable resource to help overcome grief in a healthy way. On the other hand, creating lies such as "Mom wasn't really expecting a baby, it was a joke, there was no one in the belly" or using blackmail like "If you mention your brother, you will make Mommy feel sad" can cause important psychological discomfort in both children and adolescents.

This tale comes from my personal experience of a mother struggling with the loss of my second child and the questions of my elder son and from the valuable experiences of many of my young patients, often victims of family secrets and taboos about death and mourning.

I hope that the shared reading of this story can be a helpful tool for families who are dealing with a loss, as well as an aid to recovery by enabling open expression of feelings and thoughts and to think about death without fear and without lies.

Claudia

Graphic design and illustrations by Flavia Zuncheddu.
English translation by Beatrice Sheehan.
The author thanks Antonella Bonventre and Jessica Borgogni
for their suggestions and support for translation.
The authors thanks also Carla Maria Xella and Simona Agosti
for their suggestions about the notes for parents and professionals.